FORWORD

Stand in the light when you want to speak out.
(Crow)

Our world is so full of negativity. The busier our lives become the less tolerant we become for one another and the trivial mistakes we make. Take how we drive for instance. Road rage leads people to yell profanities, gesture obscenities, and in some cases pursue violence just for cutting someone off. Holiday shopping has become another spectacle of intolerance. In shoppers' haste to be the first one in the store to buy a big screen TV, another was actually trampled to death. When did objects become more valuable than the life of another person? At what point do we stop and think for a moment before we react in such a way the consequences of our actions cannot be undone?

In writing this book, I feel compelled to remind readers of this truth; in any situation, if you turn away from negativity and focus on the positive, there is hope and love to be found. There are so many wonderful gifts and energies all around us.

They are difficult to see when we only focus on negative and material things. We each hold power to tap into these gifts and energies to help us along this life's journey in such a way it doesn't have to interfere or harm another as we move forward.

At some point in your life, it is inevitable you will suffer hardship, like the loss of a loved one and times so difficult they will rock you to your very core. These times teach us to have empathy and compassion for those around us. The reason we are here on this earth is to learn and connect with one another. It is through some of the hardest times in my life I have learned the greatest lessons. The lessons which I share in this book are to help you navigate through your own rough patches.

I have learned there is a force so strong, so loving and so caring it goes beyond anything I've ever experienced here on earth. This energy is so powerful that it transcends all things, good and bad. Whatever name you choose to call it God, Buddha, Allah, the Creator, Mother Nature, the universe etc., it is real.

In addition to the Creator and nature, I look to my Posse (a term I use to refer to my personal group of spirit guides) as my best sources of information and guidance. They have taught me that when we choose positivity over negativity, our lives become more peaceful and balanced.

We are all born with access to this power. You don't need a special talent, crisis or occasion to access this energy. It is there all the time, from your very first breath to your last. You can reach this infinite source of wisdom and guidance in your daily life in several ways. Prayer, meditation and listening to your inner voice speaking to you are some of our greatest gifts for attaining them.

Surrendering to the things in your life which you cannot change will bring you true peace. My Posse says, "Learning to listen to your inner voice guides you towards and keeps you on the path of your life's purpose".

One way of learning to listen to that inner voice is through the practice of meditation. Meditation creates a free-flowing, peaceful state of mind. Attaining such a space for ourselves, thoughts and prayers can be heard and answers received more readily.

There are many ways to meditate and achieve this desired state of mind. For some it happens while running, kayaking, knitting, quilting, coloring or engaging in an activity that brings the body and mind into balance. Some of my personal favorites include sitting quietly, taking nature walks, folding origami, practicing tai chi and meditative doodling. Depending on the day, and what I am seeking to achieve with a quiet mind and heart, I may choose any of these alone or in combination.

Reiki is an enormous part of my life; and the Reiki principle I also consider a guiding force. For me the power lies within what I will do rather than what I won't or cannot do.

Just for today

- I will let go of worry.
- I will let go of anger.
- I will do my work honestly.
- I will give thanks for my many blessings.
- I will be kind to every living thing.

I have come to learn through Reiki training and through my studies with a Native American shaman that animals, trees and all living things hold energy, medicine and powerful messages for us if we are careful enough to listen and observe them. For example, it is no coincidence if an animal you would rarely see crosses your path, it is rather trying to tell you something or make you aware of something important going on around you.

This book contains some carefully chosen, true and very personal experiences. By retelling these stories, I hope to share with you how I believe my connection to the universe and its infinite wisdom helped me, some of my Reiki clients and friends navigate through this world. These stories illustrate how choosing to be positive and to project that same energy in all you do, will have a real impact on the world and on the people in it. I hope by reading this book, it will inspire you to choose things that are positive for your life, change and learn from the negative ones, and help you find your own unique ways to connect to the universe and all that it holds for you.

THE ACORN

Listen to the voice of nature, for it holds treasures for you. (Huron)

With all the craziness going on in the world today, I feel compelled to share a special story about the tiny acorn and the mighty oak tree. After I wrote this story down, I realized the acorn had begun its communication with me many years before, when my marriage of 13 years fell apart and I became the nanny to an incredibly sweet baby girl.

My name is Abby. I am the daughter of two dedicated parents, the oldest to a brother and sister, and the mother of two grown children. I got married right out of high school and started a family shortly thereafter. My daughter Nicole came first, followed 17 months later by my son, Brian. I feel honored to be their mother and they give me purpose and happiness every day.

When my marriage ended after 13 years, I needed to find a full time job. Up until this point, I was our children's main caregiver and worked part-time outside the home. That part-time job would not be enough to support myself and two growing teenagers. With no college education and only a high school diploma to stand on, my choices felt very limited.

After scouring the newspaper for several days, an ad looking for nannies caught my eye. I drove two hours to Concord Massachusetts and filled out an eight page application. When I finished, I sat for an interview. It was then I realized most jobs would take me at least one hour from my home, and too far for a single mom and two teenagers adjusting to a whole new way of life. My children were my first priority.

As I was prepared to leave, the interviewer remembered a couple only two towns away from me had been looking for a nanny since the mother learned she was pregnant. By now, this baby girl was three months old and her grandmother was caring for her until they could find someone suitable. The woman at the agency explained they were having a hard time filling that position because no one from their area wanted to travel that far south. Just the opposite of what I was facing. This sounded like it could be a match.

I met the parents, baby girl and grandmother one week later. After a few supervised trial runs, I was hired. I stayed with this family for more than six years, during which time the family grew to include another daughter. Taking care of this baby girl was just what my broken heart needed. She was an absolute doll. I remained close enough to home and my own children; and was rediscovering my own independence and self-worth again in the process.

I remember the early days of working for this family, just sitting with her, holding her and watching her grow. When she began walking, we ventured outside to explore her big backyard. We would pick up pinecones and leaves and watch the trees blow in the wind. She was mesmerized by the outdoors. We read stories, listened to music and played. Every day was a soft and gentle experience. She seldom cried and would just look at me with her big, round blue eyes as if to say, "What's next?"

She learned to speak at an older age than most children started, and usually would nod her head when asked a question. There was no shortage of smiles or other forms of communication to get her message across when she needed to. She just absorbed all the sights, sounds and smells of her surroundings every day and enjoyed just taking it all in. The words began to flow with the birth of her sister.

In the fall, close to her second birthday and just after her sister was born, we had gone outside to play. It was a beautiful autumn day. We grabbed a yellow plastic pail to put our treasures in. She decided to fill her pail with acorns, as she loved the sound they'd make when she dropped them into her bucket. She would occasionally hand one to me, I'd hand it back and in the bucket they went. She worked so hard at filling her pail that I didn't have the heart to just dump them when it was time to go inside. We put the pail on a shelf in the garage for another day.

The next day as we headed outside to play, she led me by the hand to the garage, and pointed to her yellow bucket of acorns. I asked if she wanted them and she nodded her head "yes". Bucket in hand, she and I headed for the driveway. For the next ninety minutes she lined up those acorns to the end of the driveway. She was so intent placing them one by one in that long straight line. I left them for her parents to admire the fruits of her labor. They appreciated the display, recognizing the concentration it must have taken their toddler to complete such a task.

As she grew, the girl's fascination with acorns never changed. When she started talking, she stated that brown, like the color of acorns, was her favorite color. We would think up craft projects to do that included acorns. Once she painted a scarecrow that had an acorn for a nose. I even taught her how to make a whistle with the cap of an acorn.

Our most favorite activity was a game we invented called "Bowling with Acorns." We would find as many acorns as we could with their tops still attached, roll them down the driveway, and count the number of hops it would take for their caps to pop off. The more bounces it took, the more points you got. The points always seemed to be irrelevant. It was the excitement of counting and the anticipation of the tops flying off that brought the most joy. We played this game for years and her sister joined in on the fun. It was a favorite activity while waiting for the school bus to arrive.

It always amazed me that brown could be someone's favorite color, and a love of acorns could bring so much joy. To this day whenever I see those smooth, shiny brown nuts with their textured berets, I smile from ear to ear. I think of that sweet little girl, her adorable sister and all the fun times we had.

My life took another drastic turn. I had to move away from acorns and caring for those darling little girls when my daughter Nicole was diagnosed with cancer at the age of nineteen. After finishing up her freshman year in college, she was in a fight for her life. I took a leave of absence to be there as Nicole began a two year protocol to fight leukemia. My heart was again torn in two.

After hearing the diagnosis of leukemia, I felt devastated and petrified of what the future held for all of us. The doctors stated right up front there were no guarantees Nicole would survive the rigorous treatments that lay before her. Sheer panic ran through my body every time I was reminded of that fact with the start of each new step in treatment. Spending every day and night at the hospital with Nicole, I missed Brian and Joe, my life partner. Luckily my mother would come to the hospital and stay with Nicole so I could go home twice a week and catch up with them. I missed the girls. I would stop and see them before going back to the hospital, but it wasn't the same. It was hard to make a thirty minute visit replace the fifty hours a week I was usually there. I felt torn apart, exhausted, and constantly struggling to find balance. One day at a time was all I could handle.

The acorn however, had not finished sharing all of its secrets, with the most profound message yet to come. That message was still a few years away. First Nicole needed to get better, and second I needed to put the pieces of my life back together, again.

After many months of chemotherapy and treatment, Nicole's cancer went into remission. At the start of that long, two year journey I felt like my life was coming unglued again. It was then I found a new calling, Reiki.

Reiki is an ancient healing modality. It uses energy through gentle touch, to bring balance to the body, mind and spirit. It was a blessing to begin learning this healing art form and with daily practice, I was regaining my autonomy.

Usui Reiki, the form I chose to learn, is taught in three levels. The first level is taught and to be practiced on yourself. If you share it, it must be done with someone very close to you. The second level is a little more advanced, and you are now considered knowledgeable enough to share with others, including those you may not be familiar with. The third level is the master level; a continuation of sharing with the added ability to teach Reiki to others.

I began to feel more like myself, and after the completion of level one, a sense of order was returning to my life. Learning to let go of that which did not serve me and what I couldn't control, was freeing. It was through learning this new healing modality I was able to find balance in my life again. It helped me to be strong as I watched Nicole battle through her treatments day after day. As Nicole grew stronger, so did I.

Sometimes when the powerful anti-nausea drugs seemed useless, Nicole would ask me to share Reiki with her. I would feel a bit surprised because she has always been science minded, and show-me-the-facts kind of person. Amazingly, the Reiki always seemed to help where the medication failed.

Because Nicole couldn't explain how or why the Reiki helped with the nausea, usually we didn't talk about it. One afternoon she decided to share. Nicole stated that she wasn't sure if it was due to the fact I was her mom, and we had an established bond already, or if there was really something to this "Reiki stuff", Nicole wanted me to know she felt great after our sessions. She felt while I was an excellent mom and wonderful nanny to the girls, I should explore Reiki further. Nicole felt I had a knack of knowing just where to place my hands; no matter what was happening in that process, it seemed to work. I had been able to share Reiki with my daughter, and provide her relief from the nagging nausea.

I thought about what she said that afternoon many times. She is not one to share her deepest thoughts so randomly, and I took her words very seriously. After much consideration, I did look into it further and continued my Reiki training. I eventually became a Reiki master and taught for several years at Women and Infants Hospital in Rhode Island.

Shortly after completing my level 2 training, my inner voice and intuition really began to open up. My connection to nature and all of its components expanded daily. I noticed things I had never seen before and the world was becoming a much brighter place. It helped Nicole was feeling much better at this time and working on getting back to her life too.

It was while camping, hiking and enjoying my time outdoors in the fall of 2004 I'd begun to notice something was seriously missing. There were very few, if any, acorns scattered on the ground. No matter where I looked, those little brown nuts I was so accustomed to seeing littering the ground, were gone.

My sister has a humungous oak tree on the side of her driveway; acorns would always crackle under my tires pulling in. It wasn't uncommon for the oak tree to bean you off the head with a falling acorn or even occasionally have one put a dent in your car. I drove to her house convinced if there were acorns to be seen, her driveway was the place to find them. However, on this day, there was not one acorn to be seen or heard as I drove into the driveway. My concern quickly mounted into a growing anxiety about the disappearance of this little brown nut.

I walked up to the door and without a knock or hello, I found my sister standing at the kitchen sink with a surprised look on her face at my entrance. I asked quickly, "Hey, did you sweep your driveway?" She replied, "No." I asked, "Where in the world are all the acorns?" She stated she had noticed how exceedingly sparse they were this year, which led my worry to turn into fear. What have we done now to upset nature's balance this time? And more importantly, what are all the animals that depend on acorns as a food source going to do this winter without them?

This became a huge topic of discussion for me. I talked about it all the time. Any time I could sneak it into a conversation, I would. Joe was tired of listening to it. I couldn't remember a time, living my whole life in New England, when there wasn't a sea of acorns scattered on the ground during the autumn months. This was beginning to drive me crazy. Not knowing why there was such a lack of acorns was stressful enough, but what it could mean for the ecosystem, made it almost unbearable.

Just after Thanksgiving, I was to receive the answer I needed. Joe and I had invited a couple for an early holiday dinner one evening. It wasn't long before "the acorn topic" was brought up in conversation. Joe rolled his eyes in total annoyance at my bringing this up, again. I had already discussed this issue with my friend, but I was interested in hearing what her husband thought of the situation. Perhaps he might have something to add since he was a Boy Scout leader and outdoor enthusiast. I was confident he might have some insight since no one else seemed to know.

My friend just smiled, obviously knowing I would bring up the subject, and secretly knowing what was about to happen next. Her husband left the table and returned carrying a package. He said he thought this issue might come up and he handed me the gift. It was flat and wrapped in Christmas paper. Confused by him giving me a present, I opened it slowly. Inside was a section of the *Boston Globe* newspaper. The newspaper was not wrapping around another gift, rather the newspaper was the gift. "Read it," he said.

Written inside this paper was a story about the acorn, and the answer to my questions and concerns. I was holding it in my very hands. The article dated November 30, 2004, and the storyline was *"Acorn cycle tough to crack"*. It was one of the best gifts I've ever been given. After reading it, I placed it under my Christmas tree for all to see. I was happy to know even though there weren't many acorns lying on the ground, all would be okay. And for that one moment, there was peace on earth, at least in my world.

According to this article, scientists have noticed an oak tree's production of acorns, or lack of them, is mystifyingly synchronized. Oak trees seem to be able to control their production in nearly perfect rhythm with one another. Some scientists have even stated that these trees are smart. Scientists suggest oak trees can turn their acorn production on and off according to what is going on in the surrounding environment. If too many rodents are feeding on these seeds and not allowing enough new trees to sprout, the trees may hold off producing an abundance of them to thin out the population of animals. There were other factors considered in this article. Rainfall, weather and previous crops of acorns also seem to play a role in the following year's yield. The previous two years had bumper crops of them which made this year's lack of them seem like a drought.

I still have that article of newspaper tucked away. It was such an amazing gift, not just for me but all those who had to endure my constant chatter concerning this issue. Maybe it brought peace to them as well. I know Joe was extremely grateful. Yet, the story of the acorn goes even deeper. I will finish it in a later chapter.

GETTING TO KNOW THE POSSE

You already Possess everything necessary to become great. (Crow)

It is so difficult to pinpoint exactly when or at what age I became aware of my Posse. As a young child I saw spirit, felt things I could not explain, and heard constant chattering while alone in a room. It never frightened me and I had become so use to it I ignored it most of the time. It wasn't something I ever thought I could talk about or even explain, even if there was someone I thought would understand. It was strange but never scary.

After my Reiki training my gifts seemed to amplify. The chattering became more of a conversation that pointed directly towards me. Spirits were making more of an effort not only to be seen but to be acknowledged and my senses seemed to be on high alert. My gut feelings became less of a hunch that something was about to happen, to actual events.

I was in the grocery store one day when a stranger approached me very gently. It was obvious by the way she leaned into to me she didn't want to be overheard in what she was about to say. She was soft spoken and quietly told me I was being followed. I half smiled at her, jokingly looked over my shoulder and said, "I don't see anyone". She wasn't amused. She pointed her finger at me and said, "You know what I mean". I replied I did. She asked me if I had ever heard the word *legions.* I said I had but wasn't quite sure of its meaning. She told me to look it up sometime. She went on to say as soon as she had walked in the market she noticed the light that surrounded me and it filled the entire store. As quickly as she approached, she turned and walked away. It was so odd. I was dumbfounded. No one had ever singled me out like that before.

I finished my shopping and went home to put my food away. When I finished I grabbed my phone and looked up the word *legions.* In the Old Testament this word is given the numeric value of three thousand. In the New Testament it is used to reference a number between six thousand and infinity. That is a shocking number. If that woman was referring to my spirit guides, the Posse, I couldn't believe there were that many of them. I had never heard of a person having so many. I think most people on average have about twenty. Three thousand seemed outrageous.

I still thought it was sweet of her to take the time and have the courage to approach me and share what she saw. I just thought I was having a good day and it showed in my demeanor.

Shortly after my encounter with that woman I was given a special gift. There is a woman who uses her intuitive gifts to help people make business decisions. She is quite reputable in the Boston area. I was given a phone consultation with her shortly after I created my Reiki room. At first I was using it for my own personal meditation and quiet hideaway. I had been contemplating whether or not to open a business. Now, it is where I share Reiki with my clients.

The first thing the intuitive said she saw was I had created a space in my home or opened an office space. She then noted I did something that was very common but I had special gifts that set me apart from others who did this. I shared that I was Reiki trained. She said yes, but I was capable of so much more. She said I was supposed to be sharing this space and gifts with many people. She said,

"You must stop hiding your light. The world needs your softness and grace." She highly encouraged me to move forward with whatever plans I was making and within ten years I would be tops in my field.

She then told me something I wasn't expecting. She said, "I see you standing like the statue of liberty with a crown on your head. Thousands of energies pour from the points of this crown. These energies follow you everywhere you go. You are so protected and have so many guides you can't go wrong with anything you decide to do." She then reminded me not to let fear hold me back because the sky was the limit.

I thanked her for the advice and her time. I promised to give great thought to all she said and we ended the call.

My first thought after hanging up the phone was, what was that? Did she really say thousands of spirit guides? That couldn't be right. But then again, she was right about my Reiki room. This was the second time I was being made aware of the enormous size of the Posse.

I continued my Reiki studies in the fall of 2010 in Sedona Arizona. I became a drumming practitioner and Karuna Reiki master. Karuna is an extension of the Usui Reiki I had learned. It added more symbols and a deeper connection to the earth within my practice and use of Reiki.

During these classes, the students were taught how to take a drum journey. I had journeyed before when I studied with the shaman. Being familiar with the process and drumming, I decided to take the wild card journey. This meant there wasn't anyone or anything in particular I was hoping to connect with. I was willing to open my heart and mind and go wherever the drum beat took me. I understood this would bring me to what I needed most in order to move forward in my life.

It wasn't long after the drumming began that I was greeted by a monk. We walked together along a dark path leading downward into a cave. When we reached the bottom we exited out the right side of the cave into the desert. We were in a circular canyon with a tall flat mesa above. On the rim of this mesa were thousands of people standing at the edge looking down at us. The monk told me to wave to them. As I did I began to recognize a few familiar faces among the crowd. There was Rosemarie, a child spirit guide of mine. Then I saw Harold! Harold was the father of a woman I met at Women and Infants hospital. I met him when I was sharing Reiki with her. I only knew him posthumously. I saw chief Sitting Bull, another special guide of mine. I met him journeying with the shaman.

When I finished waving to the whole crowd of faces and had turned completely around the monk said, "This is your Posse". That's when it truly sank in and I realized my Posse did number in the thousands. I stood there for a few more moments slowly scanning the crowd one last time trying to memorize all of their smiling faces, winking and waving at me knowing I would never be able to know who they all were. It was a bit overwhelming and bittersweet to know they knew exactly who I was, yet I would never begin to know all of them.

The drum beat had changed and it was time to come back to reality. The monk and I silently walked over the proverbial bridge. I crossed over and looked back at the monk. He smiled and waved like the Posse on the mesa and slowly disappeared. I slowly opened my eyes and was back in class with my fellow students.

My first thought was still focused on the fact I possibly wouldn't get to know all of them on an intimate basis like I do Rosemarie, Harold and the Chief. I have learned I don't need to. I just need to trust that no matter who is speaking to me, they know me and what I need every moment of every day and they have my back. There was no denying their numbers now. I have seen them all with my own eyes. I might not know all of their names but they are one. They are my Posse.

COLORING PICTURES

You should water your children like you water a tree. (Hopi)

After being made aware of the entire Posse, I made it a point in meditation to try and communicate with them more on a daily basis. Some people say with consistent prayer they develop a more personal relationship with God. I wanted to have that same relationship with the Posse. I knew on occasion they were speaking to me and guiding me. I wondered what kind of relationship we would have if I made more of a conscious effort to include them in my daily life.

I was astounded at how quickly they became a part of my daily life. All I have to do is ask and they always seem ready to respond. Many times they will even make requests. I can't say I always understand why they are asking me to do these things. What I have learned is when I obey the reason for the task is revealed and a reward usually follows.

I currently still nanny for a family I have been with for sixteen years. My hours have dwindled over the years as the children have grown. I work three afternoons a week and still enjoy the time I spend with them.

I was coloring one day with the youngest child. She was about four years old at the time. We were coloring pictures of trees. She handed me a green crayon and told me to color my tree "this" color. I explained to her that I wanted to color my tree yellow and orange. It was autumn and the trees outside were beginning to change color. That led to a long, continuous string of no's and that my tree was supposed to be green. Not wanting to argue with a four year old, I colored my picture with the crayon she handed me; not without adding that people should color their pictures their own way. I then told her maybe I should get my own big girl coloring book to use. She smiled and responded, "Abby, there's no such thing as a big girl coloring book." At the time, she was correct. Adult coloring was not all the rage that it is today. Finding such a book would be difficult.

A few days later in meditation, I was told I should go to our local bookstore. I told whoever was talking to me that I didn't need or want anything from there. They repeated, "You should go." I left my room thinking I would go later if I had the time.

Later that afternoon, mumbling to myself in the car about going to a bookstore when I didn't need anything there, I pulled into the parking lot. A little irritated I was wasting my time, I went in. As soon as I got into the store I heard someone from the Posse ask me to walk straight and turn in between two book shelves. Once I turned I heard "stop". Then a voice asked me to look to my left and find a book with a brown spiral spine and remove it from the shelf. I spotted the book they were referring to, and pulled it out. In my hands was a color your own mandala book. A mandala is a round spiritual drawing. I couldn't believe my eyes.

I proceeded to the checkout, bought the book and two sets of colored pencils. I couldn't wait to show my little four year old friend this book. When I showed it to her, she was just as amazed as I was. I gave her one of the sets of pencils and said the other set was for me.

She was very careful about trying not to tell me which colors to use but couldn't help herself from making several suggestions. Over time she learned to accept my right to choose the colors I wanted to use and we spent hours coloring peacefully together, thanks to the Posse.

THE DRAGONSTONE

The more you give, the more good things come to you. (Crow)

I woke up one Saturday morning, excited to get my day underway. I had plans to meet a friend, go to a spiritual shop and out for lunch. Meditation and a check-in with the Posse first, then it would be time to get ready to go.

In meditation I was told I was going to buy a stone that day. That seemed reasonable considering we were going to a spiritual shop first. No further information was given about the stone. I finished meditation, ate breakfast and it was off for some fun.

When we got to the shop we each went our separate ways to poke through all the trinkets and collectables it had to offer. I went over to the polished stone table first. I ran my hand over the stones to see if any of them "called" to me. Nothing. I glanced over them again, read a few tags describing the stone and their meaning. None of them seemed to click with me. It was odd not to have the urge to pick any of them up and hold them. There was a lot to see, so I moved away from the table.

I browsed through the cards, dried herbs and candles. I looked at the various figurines and wind chimes. I wasn't finding anything that I was interested in purchasing. My friend had found several things she wanted to buy. I was empty handed.

I noticed a shelf across the store that had a wood carving of a crow on it. I walked over to look at it more closely. The crow is one of my animal totems. An animal totem is similar to a spirit guide only in animal form. They may appear to point something out or make you aware of something going on around you. The crow and I are good friends; both in spirit form and in nature. Many people who have spent time with me have observed their uncanniness in being in my presence and my fondness for them. It was natural for this carving to have caught my eye.

Also sitting on this shelf next to the carving was a large stone. It was shiny and had the markings of a cheetah on it. It also had a price tag of thirty dollars on it. I was hesitant to pick it up; knowing if I did I would probably have to buy it.

My friend came up behind me and we talked about the wood carving of the crow. Then she said, "Hey, do you see the stone next to it?" I said I had and asked her if she saw the price tag on it. She came back with "I think you should hold it." Then it dawned on me what the Posse had mentioned in meditation that morning. I was focused on the smaller more inexpensive rocks and I wasn't thinking their intention was for me to buy a larger stone. I reluctantly picked it up. It was beautiful and had totally different markings on the back. The other side looked like snake skin. The only other information about the stone came from a sticker on the bottom that said it was mined in Madagascar. Off to the cash register we went; she with her many treasures in hand and me with my very expensive but beautiful rock. When we left the store I told her the Posse had told me I was going to buy a stone today. It was now lunch time and we were headed to get something to eat. The plan was to go back to my house afterwards and see if we could solve the mystery as to what kind of stone I'd just paid thirty dollars for.

We had a lovely lunch and enjoyed catching up with each other, and then it was back to my house to do some investigating. We found out the name of the rock was Dragonstone. It described the spotted pattern and skin like markings exactly. We learned it is a fossil and mined in only two places in the world; Tanzania and Madagascar. It is a healing stone. The last line of the description was the most amazing of all. It is often placed in the center of drumming circles to enhance the healing power and vibration of the drum. We were amazed. As a Reiki drummer, it was truly the stone I was meant to buy that day.

Later that afternoon I drummed the stone. I figured they were going to be partners from now on so they might as well get to "know" each other. When I finished I placed the stone on a shelf in my Reiki room.

The next morning in meditation, the Posse said, "Next week when you travel with your drum be sure to take the Dragonstone with you." That was odd because when I checked my schedule after meditation there was nothing in my book about a drumming circle. I just thought they were misunderstood and went about my day.

It was later that evening I received a phone call from a woman who had heard about me from a friend. She explained her husband had been in a horrific car accident and was currently living in a rehab facility. He is part Native American and she thought he would benefit greatly from Reiki and drumming. She was inquiring to see if I would be willing to travel to the rehab place and drum with him. I told her I would be glad to. Five days later my drum, Dragonstone and I were on our way to Spaulding rehab to meet with this woman and her husband. It was an incredible healing session for all. The woman enjoyed it just as much as her husband and provided her with some much needed healing as well.

I have never regretted purchasing that stone. It has been a great addition to the drumming I've done. It looks awesome on my shelf next to the stone crow. Many have come since buying it, notice it and ask if they can hold it. I enjoy seeing the expression on their face when they discover how different it is on both sides. They enjoy hearing the story of how it came to be in my room. This is why I always listen to my Posse.

POCKET ANGEL

There is a need for obedience all around us. (Sauk)

Messages from the Posse don't always come from meditating. They often occur when I am going about my daily life.

One day I was poking around inside a bargain outlet shop. I was looking through a bin of boxes with miniature items hidden inside them. I came across a box with a wooden pocket angel inside. It didn't have a picture on the box just the words and brief description. Deciding I didn't need it, I tossed it back into the bin. Immediately I heard, "You need to buy that". I thought to myself, if I bought it I didn't know who I was supposed to give it to. They insisted I buy it. It wasn't expensive, so I did. When I got home I threw it in a bag of other such purchases I've made in the past, and tossed the bag into the closet. Learning to do what is asked, whether or not I understand why I'm doing it, has been a process. It is the lesson of obedience.

It was a year or more that had passed, when preparing for a Reiki session, the Posse had asked me to find the pocket angel. I dug through the closet and found the bag of mystery purchases and retrieved the miniature box. They asked me to give it to the client I was preparing for.

Before sharing reiki it is customary to sit and talk with the person first. It gives them a chance to express any concerns, physical or emotional, they'd like me to address during their session. Also if there are any questions they'd like me to ask the Posse.

This person wanted to know who some of her spirit guides might be. She was open to any information about them. She wanted to be able to address them personally to help her through a crisis going on in her life. I always remind them I will ask but have no control over the information they choose to share.

Shortly into our session I heard the name Magdalena. A beautiful woman with long, wavy blonde hair stepped forward and said she was one of her guides. Magdalena wore a long red velvet dress and a wreath of flowers in her hair. She encouraged my client to call upon her for guidance and support. After I finish sharing Reiki, I always take a minute to write down any messages I received for the client, and we spend some time going over them together. I had finished sharing with my client the spirit guide of hers I had met, what she looked like and her name. She found great comfort in knowing what had come through for her.

She was preparing to leave when I remembered the little box I was asked to give her. I explained I had purchased it some time ago, and was told by the Posse it was for her. She peeled the cellophane wrapper off and opened the box. Inside the box was a three inch wooden, beautifully painted angel. She had long blonde hair and a red gown painted on her wooden body. It looked just like Magdalena. We both sat with our mouths open for a minute trying to process what had just occurred. Though I have had many similar things happen in my life, this impressed me at how accurate the Posse can be. They never cease to amaze me time and time again.

I hope I always have the wisdom to listen and the will to obey their promptings. There's always a reason for everything they ask of me; I'm just not privy to the information until the time is right. That is obedience. Doing something you may not understand why at the time you are doing it, but trusting in your heart it is the right thing to do. Maybe surprising me is part of the process. It certainly helps me to keep a sense of awe and wonder alive in all I do, and a willingness to obey. I trust them implicitly. It is a bond like no other and I'm happy to share their wisdom and kindness with all who enter my circle.

THE ACORN AND THE POSSE

Trouble no man about his religion-respect him in his views and demand that he respect yours.
(Shawnee)

Several years after receiving the acorn article, the newspaper was full of headlines; so many having to do with the subject of sexuality and gay marriage. Many states were debating which were going to legalize or not. This brought many people out to voice their opinion for both sides of this subject. This topic dominated the media's attention.

My friend's daughter, who is lesbian, had suffered ridicule from others inflicting their opinions and views upon her. It was troubling for me to see her so depressed from all this controversy. I decided to discuss my feelings with the Posse.

This is what I personally believe.

I believe a higher power is in control and is one who doesn't make mistakes. To me, this higher power is the perfect creator of all things. We were purposely created to be exactly who we are, and our sexual identity is part of that. You cannot separate from that part of yourself.

Different people and religions have different views and opinions on sexuality. Some say it is against scripture in the bible for same sex couples to be together. Many say it is unnatural for two men or women to be a couple or married. They feel marriage is for sharing and creating new life. Yes, two people of the same sex cannot naturally reproduce an offspring. However, that is not the only purpose of marriage. For those who agree or disagree of same sex marriage, I offer this explanation that was given to me, from the Posse, that morning in meditation.

I started to think about my friend's daughter, and how the subject of sexual orientation is so controversial for some people. This topic creates very strong emotional responses. I felt bad for those being prosecuted by others for something I felt was out of their control. I asked the Posse if there was anything they could offer in the form of understanding that might bring some perspective to this issue. The Posse asked me to go back to the oak tree. If an oak tree can control its own acorn production due to its natural surroundings, who is to say that humans aren't immune from this same process?

Our natural resources are vanishing at an alarming rate. Global warming is the cause of rising ocean temperatures, and our polar ice caps continue to shrink with each passing year. Some scientists' say it's a natural process, others say it's the product of too many carbon gases being released into the atmosphere. Whatever the reason, these changes are evident.

Much in the same way the oak tree controls its population by limiting its acorn production, the Posse offered that maybe more people are born gay or lesbian as a way to control our own population based on our natural surroundings. Two people of the same sex cannot naturally reproduce. It was suggested that this was a response to the changes created in our environment.

Some scientists are looking into the critical phase of embryonic development during which a fetus's sexuality is determined. Among other factors, some have suggested if the mother's body temperature is off even one half of a degree, then the child will be homosexual. Look at the havoc this same temperature change has wreaked upon our oceans.

 The Posse's explanation certainly made sense to me; whenever the environment changes, all the living things within it evolve. They concluded this session with me by saying the answers I was seeking to many of life's questions could be found in nature. They asked me to pay attention for other examples that would further this explanation.

It wasn't long before a children's book, *And Tango Makes Three,* caught my eye. It tells the story of two male penguins who together try to hatch an egg-shaped rock without success. The zookeepers from Central Park Zoo decide to place a fertilized egg in their cage. They successfully hatch and raise a chick named Tango. For the nature verses nurture theorists, how do you nurture penguins to pair up with the same sex? I am not aware of any way you can nurture animals to be gay. Maybe that's just the way they were created. I reasoned this to be another example in nature the Posse was talking about.

I appreciated the food for thought from the Posse even though I don't dine on acorns. I am always grateful for their wisdom and guidance and their willingness to share with me. In sharing this story about acorns and oak trees and how it helps me to relate to others who are different from me, I'm hopeful it will encourage others to do the same. Sometimes in life there are things that are inexplicable. We are all here to learn something on this journey, and everyone's path and lessons are different. I wonder what a kinder world this would be if we were all a little more respectful towards one another as we all continue to wander through this lifetime trying to find our own truth.

SPIRIT ANIMALS

Give me knowledge, so I will have kindness for all.
(Plains Indian)

I had a session with a woman who was a shaman. I was interested in shamanism and wanted to experience what it was about.

The woman had me lie down on the floor in a room full of candles, crystals and various talismans all around me. She took time to make sure I was comfortable and asked me to close my eyes and relax. Very similar to how a Reiki session begins. I felt certain I was going to like this.

It wasn't long before my mind and body were in a deep state of relaxation. Not surprising with all the meditation practice I get. It was at this point that the spirit of a python began to slither up my left leg. My breathing changed and even stopped for a moment. The snake continued crawling closer and closer to my face. It came up to my chin and began to coil itself on my neck. It said when I calmed down and relaxed again it had three messages for me. It took several minutes for me to restore my breathing to a comfortable pace. When it did the snake began to speak again.

The first thing the snake said was that I needed to shed my skin. New things and ideas cannot come into my life while I continued to hold onto bad things from the past. To be a healer I needed to be balanced and open not bogged down with burdens, mine or others. Bad things happen to everyone to teach us something. The snake said, "learn the lessons and let go."

The second message was, "there is such a thing as being too nice". Snakes will avoid confrontation most of the time but every now and then they will strike. The snake said, "we all have the right to defend ourselves from things that will do us harm physically or emotionally. Don't be afraid to stand up for yourself". Something I have always struggled with my entire life.

The last thing the snake mentioned was how easily "rattled" I became when unexpected things would happen. I had a constant feeling of waiting for the rug to be pulled out from under me, leaving me flat on my back only to have to stand up and put all the pieces of my life back together.

It wasn't always that way, but after my ex-husband leaving so suddenly and Nicole's diagnosis a few years later; I found it hard to trust the more tranquil moments for fearing what was going to happen next.

The snake said I had very powerful gifts and they were for me to use in my own life, not just for the sake of helping others. He said very sternly, "Put your belly to the ground like a snake and feel the vibration of what was going on around you. It is hard to get caught off guard when you are aware of your surroundings. Feel it before it reaches you and you will have time to prepare yourself for whatever comes along."

With the last message delivered the snake uncoiled itself and slowly slithered down my right leg and was gone. Shortly after my encounter, the woman was done sharing her energy as well. We talked about our experiences and off I went. It left a lasting impression on me and it was all preparation for what was about to happen next in my life.

THE TALKING LADYBUG

Everything the Power does, it does in a circle.
(Lakota)

A few months after meeting with the shaman woman, I was driving to Women and Infants Hospital to give a talk about Reiki. As the Reiki instructor for the hospital it was part of my duty to do this once a month. The purpose was to inform people as to what Reiki was and entice them to take a class and learn it for themselves.

As I was driving to the office, I came to a stoplight. Waiting for the light to turn green, I happened to notice a ladybug had landed on my dashboard. This wasn't a real ladybug but the spirit of one. It was very similar to the snake that I encountered when I was with the shaman. I didn't think much of it until, just like the snake, it began to speak. Trying to keep my eyes on the road and pay attention to where I was going, the ladybug began to tell a story. It said the information was for a woman I had yet to meet. When I did, I was supposed to share this story with her.

I was really trying to focus on my task at hand. First get to the Women and Infants office safely, and then be prepared to share information about Reiki. Not all Reiki practitioners are intuitive, nor did I want anyone thinking if they took a Reiki class they would be able to see and hear the same things I did. I was always very careful to keep those things separate and my confusing happenings to myself.

I got home that evening and told Joe about the ladybug. He listened carefully and then said, "I don't know why you are getting yourself all in a fluff about this, you know how you are." I sat there for a moment with my mouth hanging open. What was that supposed to mean? He said, "This stuff happens to you all the time, it's just part of who you are." His words did calm me down a little bit, but bigger questions were looming in my mind. Why were "animals" suddenly showing up and "talking" to me? I was just getting comfortable with sharing the Posse and their messages, and now this was happening.

I did end up meeting the woman the ladybug spoke of and shared the information I was given.

She asked if we had met before, and I told her we hadn't. She wondered how I could have known this about her, and how I knew she needed to hear what I had to say. I just explained I was an energy healer and sometimes I knew things. She accepted that answer, and thanked me for sharing with her. After all, how in the world could I have told her a ladybug told me when I could hardly believe it myself?

During this time as I was trying to wrap my mind around these strange encounters, I kept asking the Posse why this was happening. They just got bossy and would give me tasks to do. The first one came one scorching summer day. The temperature was close to one hundred degrees and the humidity was in the nineties. Not a day you wanted to spend one minute outdoors. I had an appointment in the morning and the Posse said I needed to go to the pow wow that was in town afterwards. I expressed that it was too hot and didn't think I wanted to go. They strongly suggested I should make the trip.

After my appointment, I drove over to the pow wow and sat in my car with the air conditioner on full blast. I told the Posse they had ten minutes to show me where I needed to go and what I needed to do while I was there, and that was it. I sauntered over to the entry way to the pow wow and the Posse told me to go to the tents set up in the very back. Of course it was the ones in the back I needed to go to and not the ones at the very front of the event. After reaching the tents, I was completely soaked with sweat. I was hoping my trip all the way back there was going to be worth it.

Once I ducked in out of the sun, a lady greeted me and I said hello in return. We spoke a few seconds about the heat, and then the Posse told me why I was there. They asked me to find three books. I looked around and picked up three books that were scattered around that had a slight glow about them. I quickly paid the lady and back to my car I went. I passed the drummers and dancers performing, but I couldn't stand in the heat to watch. Normally I would have stood there for the entire performance. My ten minutes was done, and I couldn't wait to get back in my car and turn the air conditioning back on. It was positively miserable outside.

It was only when I was back in my car with the air conditioner on full blast that I had really looked at the books I had purchased. I noticed something odd about them. They were all written by Native American shamans.

I read all three of them in just a few short weeks. I was fascinated as to how they approached healing, energy and spirituality, they were hard to put down. I had a feeling the Posse was setting me up to begin the next phase of my journey. And sure enough, they were.

Years before, I had taken a class at a local spiritual shop. It was okay, but I wasn't overly impressed with what I had learned and done. I hadn't been back since, but I was on their mailing list. For about a year after the class I continued to get pamphlets of upcoming events, and then they stopped. It had been several years since I had gotten one, but just after finishing my third book from the pow wow, I got a flyer. The front page was dedicated to a gentleman who was a Native shaman. He was offering classes at the shop. Obviously this was what I was supposed to do next.

I signed up for his first class and took every last one he offered. The night of my first class was pretty full. He went around the room and asked each of us what had brought us to the class. When it was my turn I told him that animals were coming to me and talking to me. I explained I honestly thought I might be losing my mind. He assured me I wasn't but that I was a powerful healer and would show me what to do with the knowledge I was getting.

Most classes were eight to twelve weeks long. Usually by the end of each session, it was just the two of us for the last few classes.

I offered him a gift of tobacco after my very first class when everyone else had left. I told him I had read in a book that it was the proper thing to do. He graciously accepted the gift and spoke to me in his native tongue. He told me that the gift would be used in the manner it was received, and thanked me for my kindness.

He was always happy to spend extra time after class showing me different plants that were right at the edge of the parking lot. He told me how to collect them and what they were used for. One night, I was standing in the parking lot looking at the moon. When he came out he first thought I was having car trouble. When he realized I was looking at the moon, he stood next to me, held my hand and we said goodnight to the moon together. He again spoke in his native tongue and for that one single moment in time I actually knew what it was like to have a grandfather.

I had never experienced anything like that before or since that evening. Both of my grandfathers were alcoholics and I was never a part of their lives. I never even met my paternal grandfather. He left when my father was just four years old. This wise man filled my mind with knowledge, my soul with wisdom and for that brief moment, my heart with unconditional love. I will always treasure every moment I spent learning with him, and appreciating the impact he has had on my life. I was blessed to have had the opportunity to learn from him.

THE SONORAN DESERT

There is nothing as eloquent as a rattlesnake's tail.
(Navajo)

When we are aware of our surroundings, funny things can happen no matter where we go. Several years ago Joe and I were visiting my relatives in Arizona and we took a trip to the Sonoran Desert Museum. This was a zoo and botanical garden and it featured a hummingbird garden. We thought this would be a fun thing to do. The hummingbirds were so amazing and colorful but it was in the reptile house that a more memorable thing was about to happen.

The reptile house was a rounded building that housed all types of snakes, spiders and lizards indigenous to the dessert. Rattlesnakes are one of those animals I find both fascinating and terrifying at the same time. I enjoy having the opportunity to observe them up close as long as there's a barrier between us. I certainly would not want to meet one out in the wild.

As I stuck my face up close to the first snake's enclosure, after about a minute the snake lifted its head from its coiled body and began to move slowly to the front of its cage. We stared at each other eye to eye for several minutes. Then, I moved on to the next snake.

The very same thing happened to the snake in the next glass enclosure. I got on my knees for a closer look and the snake untucked his head, looked up and came over to the front of the exhibit. Again, I had a bird's eye view of the massive snake. It was at this point a woman standing behind me commented that the snakes seemed to like me and were all waking up when I approached their cages.

I really didn't think much about what was happening until I approached the third snake and the very same thing happened. It was a little odd that three times in a row these snakes were coming over to the front of their cages whenever I got close to take a look at them. No one else seemed to be getting the same response. I enjoyed seeing them up close, but it was time to move on. The lady was starting to bring a lot of attention to me and the fact that the snakes were reacting to my approach.

I moved on to the lizard section and the woman moved over to the spiders. It wasn't long before I heard a familiar voice call for me from across the room. "Excuse me Miss, can you come over here and wake up the spiders for my grandchildren?" Joe and I looked at one another and realized it was time to go before something really strange happened. I apologized and said we were meeting up with our family and it was time to go. Joe took my hand and said, "Let's go Snow White, you've had enough for one day".

Later in meditation, I realized that the snakes were sending me a message. I was holding onto a bunch of old stuff that was no longer serving me. Like the snake, it was time to shed the old and make room for the new things coming into my life.

Encounters like this are not coincidences. If we take a minute to reflect, there is always a message being given that has relevance in our lives. I wonder if the woman remembers that day and what would have happened with the spiders if I did go over to their enclosures. How many things are people missing because they aren't taking the time to connect and live in the moment because they are too busy or too connected to technology? I am happy to have had that experience. I urge you to do the same. Pay attention to what the universe is trying to tell you.

POSITIVE ENERGY

The more you give, the more good things come to you. (Crow)

Most of us have heard the common mantras "kindness matters," "mind your karma," and "be the change you wish to see in the world." Do you believe these sayings impact the world? Does doing or saying the right thing really matter when so many people seem to be making the "wrong" choices? I truly believe the positive energy we project has a profound impact on the world.

I have a room in my home dedicated to meditation, prayer, and Reiki. I celebrate each season, equinox and solstice with a ceremony in this room. I light candles, smudge (which means burning sage to dispel negative energy), say prayers, dance and use my drum to create positive, healing energy. My intent is not to create it for myself, but for all who come to my home for Reiki and for those beyond who are in need of healing. I drum the walls, open the windows, and try to connect to all that is around me.

Following a Friday morning tai chi class, a friend and I discussed our plans for the remainder of the day. I planned to prepare for a Reiki client, while she planned to share reiki with her friend's father, who was preparing to cross over. I wished her luck and peace for the family at their time of sadness, and we went about our day.

I went home and ate lunch. Before my client's arrival, I found I had some time to spare. I thought it would be a good time to cleanse my Reiki room and celebrate the upcoming Autumnal equinox. I performed my usual drumming, cleansing, and celebrating this time of harvest and abundance. I drummed the walls, windows, and ceiling; and sent light and love to the universe. My client arrived a short time later, and we enjoyed a lovely session.

At the next week's tai chi class, my friend asked me what I had done on the previous Friday. I thought for a moment, and before I could answer she said, "I don't know what you were doing; but the whole time I was sharing Reiki with my friend's father, I could feel you and your loving energy all around me."

At the *exact time* she shared Reiki, I was celebrating the Autumnal equinox in my Reiki room. We were both astonished. The decision to perform that ritual was random, and was performed only because I had some free time at that moment.   My intention at that time was to send comfort or light to anyone in need, not specifically to her or her friend's father. At that time, the universe felt my positive energy was needed there, this was a true blessing and lesson in positivity for all involved.

Even though my intention that day was general in nature, it found its way to a situation that needed it. We cannot control karma, but I believe this story shows how doing the right thing does have an impact somewhere in the world. How lucky I was to experience its effect first hand.

THE LAKE HOUSE

The soul would have no rainbows if the eyes had no tears. (Minquass)

A good friend of mine, who owns a lovely lake house in Rhode Island, invited me there to lead a drumming circle with a group of her friends. In addition to Reiki, I am also a Reiki drumming practitioner. I often use a large circular drum to increase the flow of energy and healing vibration over someone's body. This provides deep relaxation and is a wonderful way to touch a lot of people, especially in a group setting.

It was a perfect summer evening. Stars filled the darkening sky and the moon shone brightly over the water. It was neither too hot nor too cold. Even the mosquitos must have had their fill, and we gathered unbothered by the blood thirsty pests.

We sat in chairs arranged in a semi-circle around a blazing campfire, allowing everyone a lovely view of the lake and brilliant full moon. Once everyone settled themselves, I began to drum. I drummed each person individually and I drummed the group as a whole. As I came around to the lake, I drummed the water as well.

Water amplifies sound and vibration. My hope at that moment, which I didn't speak aloud, was anyone who could hear or feel the sound and vibration of the drum would feel at peace. It was a perfect opportunity to connect with the universe and say thank you for such a lovely evening.

We finished our drumming, and enjoyed some lovely refreshments and conversation. A delightful evening was had by all.

A short time later, my friend called to ask if I would lead another drumming circle at the lake house. I heard some concern in her voice, and asked her if everything was okay. She explained this would be different from the last circle. She asked if we could meet in the daytime instead, and explained that we would be joined by fewer people. She was holding this session for one person in particular. This woman, who she never mentioned by name, had just received some devastating news. She thought a small, quaint drumming circle with her closest friends would bring her some calm and peace as she began to cope with this personal challenge. I agreed to come.

It was another picture perfect day. The sun was shining above, there was not a cloud to be seen, and a gentle breeze filled the air. Funny how kindly the universe treated us when there was healing work to be done.

We started off by sharing what we were grateful for in our lives and offered a chance for anyone to share any concerns. Some were more general in their remarks, and others were quite open to what was bothering them. I shared an inspirational story, and then it was time to drum.

As the ladies leaned back in their chairs to get comfortable, one of the women looked up and noticed a white fluffy cloud overhead. At the center of this cloud, there was a full-spectrum rainbow shining brightly for all to see. My friend had her camera nearby, and took a picture of it. The photo still hangs on my refrigerator to this day.

Ironically, the woman who spotted the rainbow was the same person for whom we created the drumming circle. She called it a sign of hope; and she now felt no matter what happened, all would be okay.

Most astonishing is what happened next. Our hostess shared a recent experience with an intuitive. During their session, the intuitive revealed she saw a group of women sitting around a fire in the dark, near water; and that another woman was there moving her arm in a hammering motion. My friend asked, "Drumming?" The psychic answered "Yes, that's it!" How sweet and cool she was able to see our last event. The intuitive told my friend the drumming woman was magical and good things followed her everywhere she went.

My friend shared that the intuitive continued, stating everyone on the lake during our evening drumming had received a healing. I almost fell over at this revelation. My knees felt weak and unsteady, and I needed to sit down. How could that be? How could she have possibly known that? When I was drumming the water, I never spoke that intention out loud. Nor was this intuitive present that evening, or even known to me. Yet not only did she know what we were doing, she knew my personal thought and intention as I drummed over the water.

This story still amazes me to this day. I guess that is why I haven't removed the photograph from my refrigerator. It is a daily reminder for me to keep thinking big, to be kind, and to know the universe is listening and watching us.

UNCLE LOU

Do not wrong or hate your neighbor, for it is not
he you wrong but yourself. (Pima)

When my uncle passed away several years ago, it
was a sad time for his family. He wasn't an
exceptionally warm and fuzzy person that I can
remember towards me or other family members
growing up. I spent lots of school vacations at
their house, playing with my cousins, horseback
riding, and getting to experience different things
when I was younger. He worked a lot and our
contact was limited.

I always felt that was a good thing. He always
addressed my siblings and me by our last name
and announced it very militant anytime we
gathered for family functions. Very seldom
accompanied with a hello or goodbye, just
"Kennealy!", and maybe a, "What are you doing
here?" His tone and greeting always left me
speechless and feeling awkward. My body would
snap to attention whenever he spoke and I spent
the rest of the time trying to avoid him. He was
just Uncle Lou; married to my aunt, had three

children, several grandchildren, lived a long life and died.

At his wake I learned he was a navy veteran, served in the Antarctic, traveled the world, and counseled many young adults about business and life. Who knew? That surely wasn't the person I remembered. The only softness I remember seeing was with the birth of his grandchildren. They actually brought a smile to his stern face.

So imagine my utter surprise when he came to speak with me one day in meditation. As an intuitive I communicate on a daily basis with many people who have crossed over. Some I've met here on earth and others whose family members I may know. Some are just complete strangers.

After getting over the shock of seeing him standing before me, I apologized for not feeling sad about his departure. My thoughts and prayers certainly went out to his family, for I knew they missed him. I explained that it wasn't like he was an influence in my life, or that we shared any kind of bond together. Heck, we weren't even on a first name basis. He announced I was correct. He was not my father and that was not his job. I said, "Okay, then why are you here?"

He didn't apologize, but said it was wrong to address me and my siblings the way he did. Not because he didn't use my first name, but because he knew exactly how it would make me feel and react. He thought it was funny that I would be startled by his gruffness and he did it to amuse himself. He said it was wrong to do something purposely to cause another person harm or discomfort. Being negative with your words, thoughts or actions is never the right thing to do.

He continued to explain we might not understand or agree with everyone's thoughts, ideas or beliefs, but we don't have the right to make someone else's journey harder than it already is. He told me specifically that I needed to change how I was dealing with my neighbors across the street. Then, as quickly as he appeared, he was gone. No goodbye, but that was nothing new. That's just how it always was.

It took me days to process the fact that of all people, he came back to see me. He was one person I thought I would never see again. Never mind the fact that he was asking me to change and examine how I was dealing with my neighbors. I never even speak to them, so how could I be doing anything wrong? Sure, they drive me crazy but I've never acted badly towards them.

But then I began to think about how I would watch them out the window, and what I was thinking and feeling about them. The more I watched, the more it fueled the rage I felt inside, and nothing but negativity would pour out of my body. Standing in front of that window, watching what I felt was idiotic and ridiculous behavior only justified how and why I felt the way I did. Even people visiting would comment on how odd they were acting and repeat the strange things they said or did. Again, only enforcing and justifying my personal feelings. I wasn't the only one who thought the same thing, or saw them in the same light.

Day after day, I would observe their ridiculous behavior. I felt they did those things just to make me angry. I thought every time I left my front door open they took it as an invitation to perform. Yet who was the fool standing there in the window watching it?

How in the world could I ever change this pattern? They certainly aren't going to move, and we don't want to either. I look out my front window and they are all I can see.

The first thing I had to do was stop assuming they were the ones with the problem. Maybe they aren't doing things to aggravate me, but are behaving in a way that is normal to them.

Second, stop looking out the window. The minute I see them, ignore them. I've gotten very good at this. Very seldom do I even open the living room drapes. If I do, I simply just walk away and ignore everything they do. Gluing myself to that window and watching them added no value to their life or mine. If they started speaking loudly, or acting in a way I thought was calling for attention, I simply shut my front door so I could no longer hear them. Their behavior usually changes immediately when they think they don't have an audience.

Many times if I caught myself at the window and started judging or feeling negatively towards them, I would hear my uncle's voice echoing in my mind. "Remember, if you can't be a positive influence, don't be a negative one. You don't have the right to purposely make anyone's journey more difficult."

Several months had gone by and instead of just ignoring them and not sending negative energy in their direction; I was ready to be more proactive in what I could do to send positive energy across the street. This was so foreign to me where they were concerned. Before, just the thought of them would infuriate me, and now I was ready to start sending peace and understanding to the situation.

The first thing I did to begin sending positive energy was I hung tiny mirrors on fishing line on the front of my house. My thought was to reflect the peace and harmony I had created in my home outwards and I wanted that to always be my focus. Watching them flutter in the breeze and send off tiny reflections was a great thing to see coming home. They were a great reminder of where my attention should be.

Once I started to train myself to ignore them, it got easier and easier to do. If I found myself slipping, standing in the window or watching them, I had to find something positive to do to counter balance it. Now it is effortless and easy to just go about my business. My back yard has become my haven. I am rewarded with the gift of hummingbirds at my feeders, shade from the majestic oaks and a fruitful vegetable garden from the universe for my positive behavior. I will take that any day. I choose these joys in my life over feelings of hatred and endless time standing at a window watching something that just annoyed me to no end.

With karma, I believe when you do good things it's amplified in the universe. Up until this lesson I had never really given much thought to what damage was being done when I was sharing negative energy.

I cannot change or control anyone else but myself. I'm glad I was given the opportunity to change this situation for myself. I'm grateful for the wisdom and insight from my uncle. I live mindfully that it's equally important to do good and be kind as it is to control the negativity we project into the universe. We can't do one thing and not the other. I believe the impact has an equal effect upon the universe and the people in it. Doing good deeds and sharing love does not give us a free pass to let our negative actions go unchecked.

NANA

Do not judge your neighbor until you walk two moons in his moccasins. (Northern Cheyenne)

My paternal grandmother was not a very warm and loving type of person. She was very judgmental and critical. She always stated her opinion and never cared how it made anyone feel. Never did she say," I love you" or give you the impression she cared for you in any way. It's just the way she was. It was such a contrast from her mother.

I had the honor and privilege of knowing my great grandmother. I would sit on her lap for hours and talk until I had nothing to say. She would listen to every word as if there was nothing else in the world she'd rather be doing. She was a genuine and loving person. She lived long enough to see my children born and our five generation picture is one of my favorites.

I never was able to figure out why my Nana was so angry. I took a child psychology class once before I became a nanny. I had to write a paper on Nature versus Nurture. Part of my research was interviewing my Nana. I never got to the source of her irritableness but I learned a lot about her life.

She was the oldest of eight children. Her father was an electrician and he died at an early age. My Nana told me they actually had a car, which was not common in those days. She married and had four children of her own. However when my father was four years old she gave her husband an ultimatum. He needed to quit drinking or get out. Unfortunately for all, he chose to drink. With four children in tow she moved back in with her mother and raised them herself. She never divorced him or took a dime from him from that day on. I think she was a prideful person.

I always respected her for standing her ground. I know divorce was very uncommon back then but she did the best she could. She was able to travel, always had the devotion of family but just wasn't able to share her feelings. It always came out as criticism and bitterness.

The family just seemed to ignore her grumpiness the best we could and always tried to be respectful. We'd even laugh and try to make light of it whenever possible.

One day at Easter we were all outside for an egg hunt. My children are the oldest of all the cousins. My son Brian was helping one of his little cousins find some eggs. He was playing with Nathan and they were both laughing and having fun. Nana, for some reason, was unhappy with this. She proceeded to yell at Brian to stop teasing Nathan. He just ignored her. When they finished playing Brian came up on the deck where Nana was sitting. She told him "You know, you used to be my favorite but now you're nothing but a big tease." Brian came over to me quietly pretending to cry and said under his breath "I use to be the favorite and I never knew". We have always gotten a chuckle out of this story. Just making the best out of what we could. It was hard to interpret what she was upset about at times like these.

When my Nana had moved from living independently to assisted living she had difficulty adjusting to some of the people. There was one woman in particular she did not get along with.

My parents had picked her up to take her out for the day. After doing some errands they brought her back to their house for some lunch. She told my mom she might as well tell her something because she was bound to find out anyways. She told my mom she was tired of this woman and got up, walked over to her and slapped her in the face. My mom told her she couldn't do that. She had no right to hit anyone. When they brought my Nana back to her home they spoke with the staff and tried to smooth things out. They in turn agreed to try and keep them separated.

Shortly after this incident we were discussing Nana's birthday and racking our brains on what to buy her. My brother jokingly suggested boxing gloves and silk shorts. We all laughed hysterically at his suggestion. He never missed an opportunity to spar at her behind her back any time she walked by. It was another one of those inside jokes born from a moment of irrationality.

My last harsh memory of her was her last Easter with us. Her sister and I were waiting for my dad to get back from picking up my Nana. I saw my dad pull in the driveway and we moved to the kitchen to greet her. I extended my arms to give her a hug and wish her a happy Easter and she shoved me backwards and yelled, "It's not a good day!" I actually took a few steps backwards into the stove from her push. I told her I hoped she had a nice visit with her sister and made no attempt to communicate with her for the rest of the day. Sadly, I left at the end of the day without even saying goodbye. She made it clear she was in a mood. Always best not to poke the bear in its cage.

Several days after celebrating her 96th birthday, complete with family, cake, flowers and balloons she was in the hospital. It was then she made the announcement she was tired and ready to go. She no longer wanted to be here on earth. No extra measures were to be taken and she was refusing to eat any more. Everything was done to keep her comfortable and happy until her time here was done. My mother brought her all her flowers and balloons to her room so she had something lovely to look at.

I chose not to go and visit her during her brief stay in the hospital and nursing home to say good bye.

I am not good with that sort of thing and did not want to upset her. Instead I chose to remember her eating cake, laughing with her sister and playing with the balloons I had given her for her birthday. These memories were few and far in between and I didn't want to chance an outburst.

The following morning after she was admitted to the hospital, I decided to send her some Reiki. I prayed and asked that her passing be peaceful from this life to the next and that all of her wishes would be honored in her final hours. My parents went several times a day to check on her and her daughter came from Arizona to say goodbye.

After I had sent Reiki, my mother had called and asked if I had gone to see her. I told her I hadn't. She asked if I had sent her Reiki and I said I had. She told me my Nana told her I came for a visit. She tried to explain to my mother that she could only see me when her eyes were closed, but when she opened them I was not in the room. She felt I had visited her, but couldn't remember seeing me with her eyes open. That meant the world to me.

As far as she knew I worked as a nanny. She wasn't aware, to my knowledge, that I was a Reiki

Master or intuitive. Some of my Reiki training had taken place in Arizona. My aunt and uncle live there. As far as she was concerned my trips out there were to visit them. Some of them were. I don't know whether or not she would have understood Reiki or the concept of what I did. I will be forever grateful she felt what I had done that day and her passing was peaceful. I didn't feel guilty or remorseful for not visiting with her before she passed because in a way, we did. In her heart, maybe she understood what I had done. It is a beautiful thing to think that was the last thing we shared together and on some level she loved me.

Karma, trying to do and say the right thing no matter how you think it will be received. Doing things just because it seems like the right thing to do can bring joy and happiness into your life and the life of others.

PLANTS

All plants are our brothers and sisters. They talk to us and if we listen, we can hear them. (Arapaho)

Not just people and animals respond to loving energy, but plants do as well. Most people have had an experience with a pet or animal, but plants respond to us also, it's just noticeably slower. You have to be more patient with plants, but their messages are of equal importance.

For St. Patrick's Day one year Joe bought me a bamboo plant. This plant has gone from a petite nine inch plant to now standing around five feet tall. Some of the plants I have an attachment to seem to be attached to me as well.

The bamboo lives in a big pot of rocks and water on our dining room floor. It needs very little care but it likes a lot of attention. If I don't touch it often and fuss over it, it starts to turn yellow. The more attention it gets, the greener the leaves are. I have only come to notice this after I went to Arizona to study and was gone for two weeks. Joe was unable to come, so he was left in charge.

I figured he could handle giving the plants a little water about half way through my trip and all would be well. We've traveled before and the plants have always managed to be fine with no one home to care for them.

You can imagine my surprise when I walked in the door from my trip and found my bamboo had turned completely yellow. I asked Joe what happened and he said, "Nothing." I asked why my bamboo was yellow. He said he didn't know but maybe it just missed me was the answer he offered.

I went straight to work caressing its leaves and I chanted some of the new Reiki symbols I had learned. Within five days the bamboo was back to its vibrant green color and I had learned a new lesson about plants. How odd to think a plant could "miss" someone or at the very least recognize a shift in energy. To further exemplify this message, my ivy plant that lived in my kitchen window had the same reaction.

My sister had given me a beautiful heart shaped ivy plant for helping her and her family move into their new home eight years prior to my trip. It too had turned almost completely yellow in my absence. After the same treatment I gave the bamboo, the ivy made a full recovery as well in about two weeks. A good friend of mine who is a professional gardener often commented how beautiful my ivy was. She said it was very difficult to keep them indoors and she couldn't believe how long I had kept it for.

These plants are accustomed to receiving a lot of attention because they are placed in my favorite spots in the house. I'm forever touching them, pulling off dust and clipping all the dead leaves constantly. That was the only difference between the care I gave them and Joe. I never really thought about plants and energy until this happened.

Around the same time I was going through this with my plants, a friend of mine's daughter had decided to do an experiment in science class involving plants. She had gotten two plants roughly the same size and type and wanted to see how they reacted to energy. One plant she kept in a window watered it and gave it the basics it needed to survive. The other she kept in her bedroom. She gave this plant a lot of attention. She played music for it, she talked to it and basically it became her friend. She did this to see if there was a difference between the two plants. Just as I had found out, the plant that was her friend had grown and thrived under her watch and responded to her loving energy. The window plant had remained virtuously unchanged in the few months of her experiment, growing a mere half an inch, while the other plant grew an extra three inches.

My bamboo continues to thrive in the dining room but the ivy died after twelve years. Maybe it was my imagination or maybe it was real, but one morning when I was standing at the kitchen window, I knew the ivy was going to die. It was green and it looked okay, but somehow I knew it was coming to the end. I had even told this to Joe. Sure enough, within one week all the leaves started turning brown and it shriveled up and died. I buried it in the garden and returned it to the earth and was grateful to have had it in my life.

I am thankful I had this experience with them. It has taught me more about energy and sharing it with all living things. Plants may not have feelings, but they do respond to energy just as humans and animals do. It just happens a little slower and you need to have the patience to watch for it. The world is full of so many wonderful things if you are diligent enough to try and connect with it. In order to do so, we must disconnect every now and then from our technological devices otherwise you will never see the wonder that surrounds us.

A good photographer is able to catch the beauty that surrounds them because they are patient, waiting for the perfect light and moment to snap their picture. When everything in your life is done in haste, joy is diminished and it's hard to remember the events that have occurred. We must slow down our bodies and let our minds enjoy the beauty of this world if we wish to find peace and balance in our lives.

CONNECTING TO ANIMALS

Every animal knows far more than you do. (Nez Perce)

Pets add such joy to so many lives. This is one of the easiest ways to connect with nature. Personally I am a big fan of Beta fish, also known as Siamese fighting fish, and I have cared for several over the years. Each one was special in its own way, some even displaying different personality traits.

One fish in particular I thought was extremely special was a beautiful blue female I named Luna. She was so fun to observe and care for. She loved having her water changed in her bowl and seemed to enjoy having various objects decorating her bowl. I rotated different ones for her in and out on a regular basis. She was particularly fond of her miniature Easter Island statue. She enjoyed rubbing up against it and resting on the bottom of it.

Shortly after choosing her at the pet store, another handsome male had caught my eye. He was bright orange-red with long flowing fins. His name was Scaredy-cat. This poor fish spent most of his time hiding in the roots of the plant I had growing on top. He seemed to hate being looked at, and I never saw him eat anything for at least one month after buying him. This worried me to no end. Every morning I expected to come downstairs and find him floating belly up.

One day after giving both Luna and Scaredy-cat a "bath", I decided to place their bowls next to each other so they could see one another. Scaredy-cat lived on our dining room table and Luna lived on the coffee table in the living room. It was the first time in over a month I had seen Scaredy-cat swim and show any interest in doing anything but hide in his roots. I left them together for about one hour and then put Luna back in the living room. He was never the same after that first playdate.

He became a totally different fish. He started to greet me in the morning when I sat down to read the newspaper. I would feed him and watch as he began to eat whatever I put in his bowl. It was amazing. I had never seen such a change or anything like this in all my life. Needless to say, their playdates became a regular part of our routine. Once or twice a week I would put them side by side to see each other and communicate.

Scaredy-cat even built bubble nests for his lady love. It was a plutonic match made in heaven. He eventually let it be known he wasn't fond of having his bowl changed around. He loved his roots and leaf hammock, something that he actually slept on, and that was it. Anything else would send him pouting and hiding in his roots. Luna, being such a happy go lucky kind of fish, sure taught him a thing or two. It was so sweet to think she actually had an impact on his life.

After a couple of years, Scaredy-cat passed away. I put Luna next to his bowl so she could see for herself. Do fish grieve? I can't answer that question but I can say Luna seemed different after their last meeting. I thought maybe she was coming to the end of her life too. After all, I had them both for quite some time.

A trip to the pet store to buy a new decoration for her bowl, led to the purchase of something extra. A baby female beta had caught my eye. For lack of imagination, I decided to call her Baby until I could come up with a better name. I never did. Baby and Luna lived side by side on the coffee table in the living room. Luna seemed to be back to her old self having this little one swimming around next to her.

Life was good with the girls. Baby was growing and getting bigger by the week. She lived in a fish bowl I mounted onto an upside down clay flower pot I had painted red. It looked like a gumball machine. Because she was so small, I had very fine gravel at the bottom of her bowl so she wouldn't get stuck under anything. Eventually, I thought she was big enough and I replaced the gravel with glass marbles to look like gumballs. Everyone thought it was cute.

One morning about a month later, I had come downstairs, turned on the tea kettle, and headed for the living room. I said good morning to the girls, who were both happily swimming in their bowls, and began to check my emails waiting for the water to boil for my tea. I made tea, and usually after I finished my first cup, checked my schedule and watched the weather on TV, it was feeding time. Not this morning.

After I had resettled on the couch with my cup of tea, Luna started swimming across the top of her bowl making an unusual smacking sound. It was so strange. I had never seen her do this before. Back and forth, over and over and it went on for about five minutes. I got up thinking she wanted to be fed and sprinkled some food into her bowl. She didn't even look at it. She was a plump old girl, and she loved her food. She just continued doing her laps back and forth. I thought while I was already up I might as well feed Baby too. I looked and looked, no Baby. What was going on?

I've got Luna swimming like an Olympic champion in one bowl and now I can't find Baby in hers. I am starting to get a little panicked about not being able to see Baby. Then I looked straight down into the bowl and I saw her. She was trapped beneath the clear marbles, and she was not moving. Total panic washed over me. What do I do now? If she was not yet dead, she would be for sure if I started moving the marbles around trying to free her.

I rushed her in her bowl over to the kitchen sink. Still in a panic and not sure of what to do next, I realized that I needed to first calm down. I took a second to close my eyes and take a deep breath. It was then I heard, "Take two fingers and gently wiggle the marbles near her." Without hesitation, I took two fingers, lined them up, closed my eyes and hoped for the best. I gently wiggled the marbles and when I opened my eyes Baby was swimming at the top of her bowl. I couldn't believe it! She looked no worse for the wear.

After an immediate change back to the small aquarium gravel in the bottom of her bowl and putting the marbles away, she was back in her place on the coffee table next to Luna. I sprinkled some food into Baby's bowl, and guess who else had decided she was also hungry? I guess the fish Olympics had ended while I was changing Baby's bowl, Luna had won the gold medal and had worked up quite an appetite with all her swimming and smacking that morning. What an uncanny morning of events.

Did Luna really know Baby was in distress? Was she doing those things to get my attention? It certainly seemed like it. And even though life seemed to quickly go back to normal for them, my mind continued racing for the rest of the morning trying to make sense of it all.

As an intuitive I am accustomed to hearing, seeing and feeling things that others don't. I know someone from the Posse was giving me specific instructions to free Baby from the marbles. That isn't the part of the story I found baffling. It was my relationship with a beta fish I called Luna. She really was amazing. How she was able to help Scaredy-cat and now Baby I will never know. She was like no other fish I've ever cared for.

Baby and she lived side by side for about another year. Baby grew and eventually was big enough to get all of her marbles back. Believe it or not, Baby actually passed on first. About two months after Baby passed, Luna started to really change. Her swimming was different. It was much slower and seemed to require a lot of effort. She would come up to the surface of the water to eat, and would often miss the pellet she was aiming for. She was truly getting old. I made sure her water temperature was on the warmer side, and she had plenty of her favorite foods. Her beloved Easter Island statue was always in her bowl.

I sat down one evening to watch television with my very special aquatic friend and I knew she was waiting for this moment. Before I even turned on the television, I moved onto the carpet and watched her for a few minutes instead. It was then she began to swim on one side. She would wiggle on and off for the next ten minutes or so and then she was still. There was emptiness in the living room that couldn't be filled. I'm sure some would think it silly to cry over a dead fish, but she was no ordinary fish to me. If Scaredy-cat and Baby could talk, I'm sure they would've said the same thing.

This story is an example of what we can notice and experience when we take the time to nurture and pay attention to our surroundings. Any time I invested in caring for and watching these fish I certainly got back three fold. What are you missing in your life because you are not energetically plugged in to the people and world around you?

ANOTHER SPECIAL ANIMAL

Thoughts are like arrows: once released they strike their mark. Guard them well or one day you may be your own victim. (Navajo)

A Reiki client had come for a session one day and from the moment she arrived it was clear she was very upset. This was only her second visit and we were just getting to know one another. I knew a few things about her like what she did for work and that she had children; beyond that, not much else.

We went downstairs to my Reiki room, sat down and I handed her some tissues. She took a moment to catch her breath and shared she had just lost her beloved pet. She never revealed what type of pet it was but did say she was receiving a lot of negative and disheartening comments from her coworkers about it. This puzzled me because so many people are animal lovers and have pets of their own. Some of the comments included "just get over it" and "it's no big deal". Add to the confusion that it had been less than a week since her pet had died.

Trying to bring some comfort, I said grief is different for everyone and not knowing her coworkers I wasn't sure why they were acting that way. I wanted to begin our session as soon as she was ready to see if the Posse or my intuition could shed some light on this situation.

It wasn't long after she laid down on the table her breathing calmed into a slow steady rhythm, the tears stopped rolling down her cheeks, and her body relaxed underneath my gentle touch.

It was then the first message came in. I saw a white fluffy ball of something looking under a sofa. It didn't have a tail like a cat or dog, but it was clearly some sort of animal. A few seconds later its head popped out from underneath the couch and I realized it was a chicken. What in the world was a chicken doing in the house and looking under the sofa? Once I identified what type of animal it was, it strutted over to a woman who scooped it up into her arms and that was all I saw of the chicken.

This is a normal occurrence for me when I am sharing Reiki to see, hear and feel many unusual things. It doesn't always make sense the moment it's coming through, but when I am done these things tell a story. When I am through sharing Reiki I write all of the things I experienced down, and when the client is ready I do a reading and interpret the messages for them.

These messages are powerful and only serve to enhance the healing experience. The Reiki works on the physical aspect of the body. The intuitive part works with the Reiki on the emotional and spiritual side. It is great for shedding light on things that are complicated or issues the person is struggling with.

Other messages were given that day, but it was the chicken that carried the biggest one. This message brought the most comfort.

My client slowly arose from the massage table, sat back in her chair and had some water. This gave me a chance to think about what I saw and put the pieces together of what I had witnessed. When she was ready, I began my reading.

I again expressed my sympathy at the loss of her pet and hoped the Reiki brought some comfort and peace. She said it did. I asked her if by any chance the pet she lost was a white chicken. Tears welled up in her eyes again and she muttered a soft yes through her gentle sobs. I asked if her mom had left the physical world and she nodded her head yes.

Her coworkers couldn't relate to her loss of a chicken. They didn't understand how someone could love a chicken, never mind letting it live in her house. It wasn't your ordinary pet.

This chicken had a crate and she was a neat and tidy sort of person. She was diligent in cleaning up after it. More importantly this was a pet she had shared with her mom who had passed several years earlier.

This pet, like my Luna, was an amazing creature. It played fetch, liked to cuddle on the couch and even watched movies and ate popcorn with her mom and herself. Saying goodbye to this chicken, in a way, was like saying goodbye to her mom all over again.

I mentioned when I saw the chicken, she was looking under the sofa. She said that was where most of her tin foil balls ended up after they played fetch. I said there was a gift from her under that sofa waiting for her to find when she got home. She doubted it because she said she had done a thorough cleaning after the chicken had died. She had moved furniture, removed the crate from the house and collected her remaining feathers that had molted. She and her mom would wash them and keep them in a large glass jar.

I could only mention what I saw and relay the message as it was given. We finished our reading, she dried her remaining tears for the moment and was grateful she had come that day. She said knowing her chicken was with her mom made all the difference in her moving forward. She was happy to know someone understood her feelings, even if her coworkers didn't.

Only about one hour passed after she left when my phone rang. It was my client on the other end. She wanted me to know when she left she went straight home after our session. Reluctantly, and doubting she would find anything she had to look under the sofa. There she found two white feathers waiting for her. The joy in her voice was a special gift for me. The feathers were an everlasting one to her from her incredibly loved chicken.

This story is another example of how important it is to be kind and compassionate. Even if you are unsure of where that person is coming from, your actions can either help or make the situation worse. Why wouldn't you choose the better of the two? Her coworkers seemed to dismiss her grief because after all, to them it was just a chicken. Was my grief any different because my pet was a fish?

When we judge someone or a situation quickly and without thinking, chances are we don't comprehend the whole story. In this case, her coworkers missed the part that it wasn't just the chicken she was mourning. Usually, when we take the time to try and understand exactly what is going on our reaction is different and more appropriate. This is all the more reason to try and be mindful of our words and intentions.

I do not claim to have all the answers as to how energy works, nor am I a scientist of any sorts. I can only relay the experiences I have had and have been witness to.

I believe the only things that cross over with us into the afterlife are love and the relationships we have created with one another. In the end it will not matter how much money we made but what we chose to do with it. It won't matter how many material things we collected, the clothes we wore or the cars we drove, but how many true friends and family members we had and how we treated them. It will matter when we were given the chance to do something kind, we took the opportunity to do so; and when we were treated less than we deserved we chose understanding over revenge.

I believe we need to learn to be accepting of others in order for others to accept us for who we are. We all wish to be understood. If everyone is talking and shouting their beliefs and no one is listening, what's the use?

When you choose kindness, positivity and peace not only is it amplified in our own lives but the lives of others and all who share this planet with us. I hope this book is an inspiration for you to be a positive influence and create harmony for yourself and others. If you do this, the world will be a better place for all.

A HORSE NAMED APPLE

When we show respect for other living things, they respond with respect for us. (Arapaho)

My lake house friend also owns a farm in Chepachet, Rhode Island. Her animals are not only part of her livelihood but she loves and cares for them like a mother would her children. They are all very special to her and she knows them inside and out.

It was out of desperation one day that she called asking for my help. Her horse named Apple, who was in her thirties, was having trouble eating and she couldn't figure out what was going on. She had some problems with her teeth given her advanced age, but she didn't think that was the reason she wasn't eating. Her biggest concern was Apple's age and she thought she might be coming to the end of her life. She wanted me to see if I could somehow connect with her horse and find out what was going on.

I told her that anything was possible but I couldn't make any promises. I had never been asked to do this before and I thought it might be pushing my limits a bit too far, but I agreed to try. I told her I would call right after and let her know if anything came through.

I went downstairs to my room, lit a white candle, asked the Posse for their help and called Apple's name. After only a minute or two guess who came trotting in.

I was amazed at how easily I was able to get her to come to me. I asked her what was going on and I heard that her neck and throat were hurting. I asked if that was why she wasn't eating and the reply I heard was yes. I explained her mom was worried about her and wondering if it was time for her to cross over. The response I heard was," it wasn't her time yet." I told her I would let my friend know and off she trotted.

I called my friend immediately after this encounter and relayed the information I had heard. She said she would put a call into the vet. The vet came out the next day and put a scope down the horse's throat. Sure enough there were ulcers in Apple's throat. The vet said it looked raw and would make eating and swallowing painful.

He prescribed some medicine and within a few days Apple was feeling better.

We were both amazed at what had occurred. Only years of training and my friend's belief in me gave me the confidence to even attempt such a thing. I was grateful to be able to help such a dear friend and her beloved horse.

Several months had gone by and again I got a phone call from my friend concerning Apple. She was not feeling well and asked if I could work up some magic again and check in with her and see what was going on. I jokingly stated, "Of course I could do that", with all the confidence that I had done this a hundred times before. Kidding aside, I told her I would do my best.

I went down to my room, lit a candle, asked the Posse for guidance and invited Apple to come and visit. It wasn't long before she appeared only this time the moment I saw her, my whole body began to ache. I hurt all over. I asked her what was wrong. A one word answer was replied, "Lyme." I realized she must have been bitten by a Lyme tick.

I called my friend and relayed the information I was given and told her how my body ached. She said she would call the vet right away and have a blood test done. Sure enough the results showed Lyme disease. She was treated with antibiotics and she was feeling better in a few weeks.

The next call I received from my friend concerning Apple was of a happy nature. My friend had arranged for Apple to go to a pasture for a day to graze on some fresh green grass. The only problem was Lady A associated the trailer with going to the vet's. It was difficult to load her onto it. Usually it took my friend and her husband to lock arms behind her flank and push her on to it. She was wondering if I could have a talk with her and explain that she had something fun planned for her and it would be helpful if she got onto the trailer nicely.

Could I? What kind of question was that? It was me she was talking to. Apple and I were now BFFs and we were enjoying our girly chats. I told her I would be glad to give it a try. I was enjoying the results of these little trials.

I began my ritual. Down the stairs I went, lit the candle, called the Posse, and whistled for Lady A. I spoke to her softly and told her that she had a special day planned for her and she needed to cooperate getting into the trailer. I told her she had nothing to fear and it wasn't a trip to the vet. She would like it and it would mean the world to her mom if the trip started off smoothly. No reply was given, but I know she heard what I said.

The next morning came; they pulled the trailer up and dropped the back door down. Much to her and her husband's surprise, Apple walked right onto the trailer without a single hitch. It was as if she knew where she was going and she had nothing to fear just as I told her. She had a wonderful day eating grass and frolicking around the pasture.

As a thank you for all the work I had done with Apple, my friend gave me a beautiful black and white photo of her. I placed it on the landing between the floors of my house so I could see it every morning when I went downstairs. One morning descending the stairs I looked at her photo and heard the message, "It's time for me to go." My heart sank. I knew at that moment Apple was getting ready to go. I didn't have the heart to tell my friend. I knew she would know soon enough.

Only two days had gone by when I got the call. The vet was on his way to put Apple down and she just wanted to be sure she was doing the right thing. I assured her she was and that I knew a few days prior. She knew in her heart it was but it seemed to bring some comfort coming from me, knowing my relationship with Apple.

I called my friend the next day to see how she was feeling. We talked and I thanked her for having the faith in me to connect with Apple. It was just as beneficial to me as it was to her. A true win-win situation. She was able to get Apple the proper care for what was ailing her and I learned I could communicate with animals at will, and not just the ones who came bearing messages. Such an amazing gift I never would have known I had otherwise. An everlasting gift from a special horse; it cultivated a precious friendship between us and one with her owner.

MY DAILY LIFE WITH THE POSSE

When we understand deeply in our hearts, we will fear and love and know the Great Spirit. (Oglala Sioux)

It has taken me years to learn to trust the Posse and follow the many crazy requests they make on a consistent basis. I have come to know if I am obedient and do what they ask of me, great rewards are sure to follow. I can't say I always understand the reasoning behind each of these promptings, but if I trust them, follow their instructions and listen with my heart, our bond only grows stronger.

The Posse has laid a trail of bread crumbs for me to follow through this journey that is my life. They have led me step by step, helped me and all those they put in my path. My life is blessed, balanced and I know I can tackle anything that comes my way.

I urge you, the reader, to find simple ways to be kind and mindful of your words and actions so that you too will have a peaceful, happy and balanced life. Remember you were born with your own set of guides and the universe wishes to speak with you as well, if you will take the time to listen.

My hope in writing this book, and you reading it, will help to make this world a better place for everyone in it and know the infinite possibilities that can happen when we love one another.

94483367R00064

Made in the USA
Lexington, KY
31 July 2018